Our Garden

Susan M. Guthrie

Rigby®

HOUGHTON MIFFLIN HARCOURT

www.Rigby.com
800-531-5015

This year in school, I am keeping a journal of our garden at home. Our family grows a garden every year, just like we did back home in Laos.

I am planting seeds with Grandma.

Early Winter

It's still snowing outside. The air is very cold, but today Grandma and I planted tomato seeds. The seeds will grow on our sunny windowsill.

There's a **thermometer** on our back porch that shows the **temperature.** Today it's at 40 **degrees.** It's too cold to plant seeds outside, but it doesn't get as cold as **freezing.**

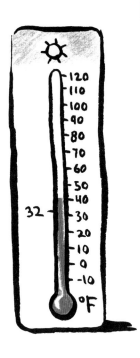

My teacher said 32°F is when water turns into ice. She told us to write the word degrees as °. She also said to write **Fahrenheit** as F instead of writing the whole word.

Late Winter

The seeds have grown in our warm house. The days outside are getting warmer, but the nights are still too cold for planting. Grandma said we must wait until the ground is warmer. Then we'll put the plants in the garden.

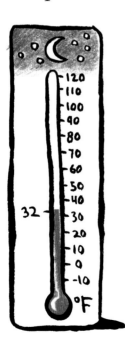

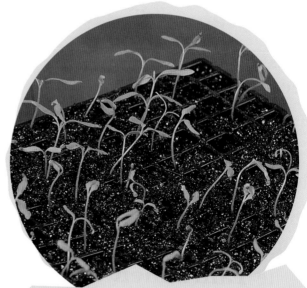

The plants are growing!

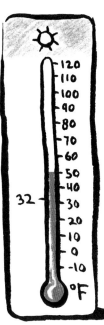

Today the temperature got up to 50°F. As the temperature gets warmer, the **liquid** in the thermometer gets higher. Soon it will be time for the vegetables to begin growing in the garden.

Early Spring

I plant the vegetables in rows.

Grandma said it's time to plant the watermelons, sweet potatoes, and onions outside. We planted sweet potatoes every year when we lived in Laos, too.

The nights are getting warmer. Now the lowest temperature at night is 48°F. That's 16 degrees above the freezing temperature, which is 32°F.

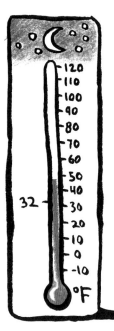

I can't wait to eat these watermelons after they grow!

Middle of Spring

The watermelons, sweet potatoes, and onions are doing well. The other plants in the garden are getting taller, too. Grandma said the soil is now warm enough to plant corn and cucumber seeds. I remember planting corn in Laos.

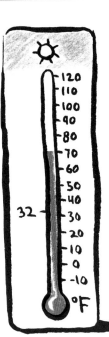

The days are getting warmer, and every day the liquid in the thermometer gets higher and higher. Today it was 70°F. Now most nights don't go below 52°F. That's 20 degrees above the freezing temperature.

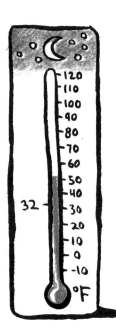

Grandma and I planted more vegetable seeds.

Late Spring

Grandma shows me how to cook the vegetables.

We picked the first vegetables of the year. Grandma chopped up the sweet potatoes and onions and made some soup.

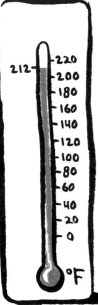

My teacher said that water boils at 212°F. That's very hot! It's a good temperature to cook vegetables, but it's much too hot to eat. Grandma tells me to put an ice cube in my soup to cool it off so that it is safe to touch or eat.

Middle of Summer

I'm picking tomatoes!

The garden is full of ripe vegetables. Sometimes we pick them early in the morning, and sometimes we pick them in the evening. It's too hot during the day to be out in the garden.

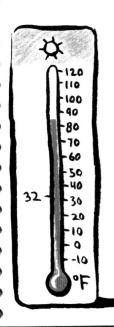

Today it was 85°F, and last night it was 70°F. I like warm nights. Grandma says the vegetables like warm nights, too! I'll remember these days and nights when the temperature drops again next winter.

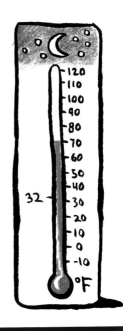

Early Fall

The days are still warm, but the nights are getting colder. We saved the seeds from some of our vegetables. We'll have fun planting them in next year's garden.

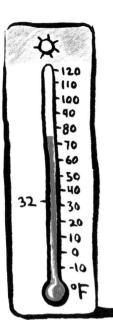

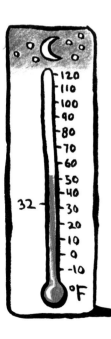

The high temperature today was 75°F, and it was 51°F last night. Soon the liquid in the thermometer will go lower and lower. The earth will cool down and get ready to rest for the winter. Then next spring, we will begin planting again!

The watermelon is great!

Glossary

degrees   numbers on the thermometer scale

Fahrenheit   a temperature scale

freezing   the temperature when water turns to ice (32°F)

liquid   something that flows freely like water

temperature   the degrees of hot or cold

thermometer   a tool that measures temperature